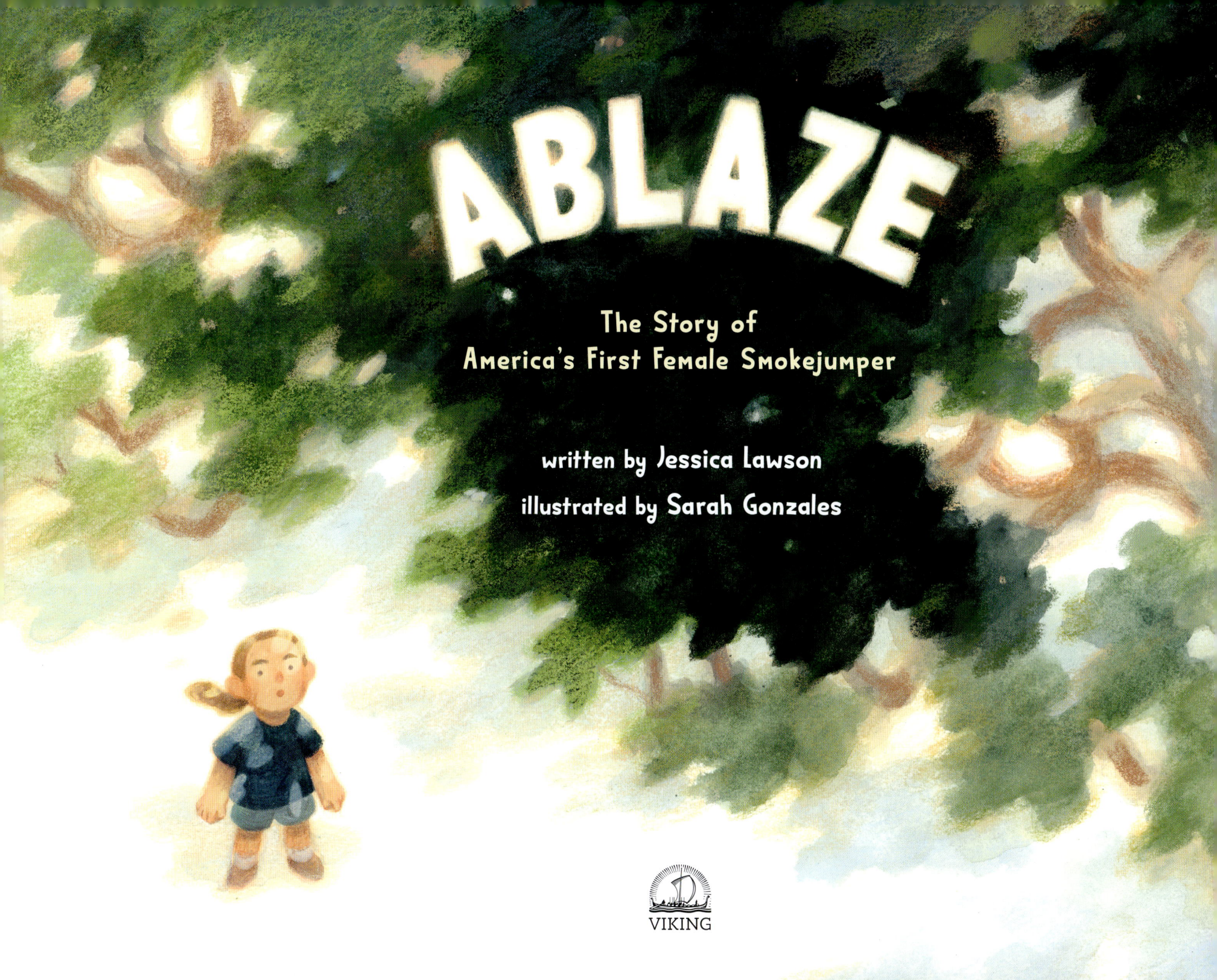

ABLAZE

The Story of
America's First Female Smokejumper

written by Jessica Lawson

illustrated by Sarah Gonzales

VIKING

ONCE, there was a very small girl.
And a very tall tree.

Climbing into the tree was easy,
but getting back to the ground . . .

She looked down at the forest floor far below.
She held tight to the tree's sturdy branch.
Her skin prickled. Her heart beat as fast as the wind.

She was nervous to let go
(and also a little excited).
One, *two*, *three*,
she whispered.
And then . . .

Deanne Shulman jumped.

Deanne loved being outdoors.
Driving with her family to the Salton Sea
for sailing and to the Sierra Nevada mountains
for backpacking.

Sea spray salty in her mouth.
Sun searing hot on her face.
Raindrops tapping on the tent.
Stars twinkling in the night sky.

Her parents carried the heavy packs.
Deanne and her brother carried the lunch.

As Deanne grew older,
her love of nature grew as well.

So when the snowpack was sparse in the
California mountains,
and the heat rose each fire season,
and the blazes burned near and far,
she noticed.

She knew wildfires could be a good thing.
Burning old and dead plants
spread nutrients to the forest floor,
creating rich soil for new growth.

But not all wildfires were good . . .

Some were dangerous.
Lives were lost. People. Animals.
Houses full of memories, too.

Deanne applied for a job with the United States Forest Service, where her brother had worked on trail crews.

He built and maintained trails so that others could enjoy nature as much as their family did.

She was hired—not to work on a trail crew like her brother.
She was hired to fight fire.

She learned fast and the job fit well.

Hard physical work. Camaraderie
with crewmates. Being outdoors.
All things that fueled her heart's fire.

She worked on wildland crews, where brush trucks traveled remote roads to access wildfires. Crewmembers hiked in with tools and supplies, clearing brush and branches that might make the fire spread.

She worked on hotshot crews where she fought faster fires and took bigger risks.

Muscle aches and heavy, protective clothing.
Sweat salty in her mouth.
Short naps with no sleeping bag.
Curled up, waking like a big ball of dirt.

One-hundred-degree heat and
twenty-four-hour workdays.
Air scorching hot on her face.
Smoke masking the light of sun and stars.

Yet Deanne had found her spark.

But there was still one dangerous job
that she'd never had a chance to try . . .

Smokejumper.
Planes and parachutes.
Free falls and hard knocks.
Far from access roads that
any brush trucks could reach.
All to be the first line of defense
when it came to fighting fires.

There had never been a female
smokejumper in the United
States Forest Service.
Did that stop her?

No.

At the age of twenty-six, she took the first
of the required physical tests:
seven pull-ups
forty-five sit-ups
twenty-five push-ups
a 1.5-mile run
in less than eleven minutes.
No problem for Deanne.

She was ready for the next test:
3.5 miles over rugged terrain,
115 pounds on her back,
in three and a half hours or less.

But she never got the chance to try.

Instead, she was pulled aside
for looking too small.
At the time, being five feet, five inches tall
and at least 130 pounds were the minimum
United States Forest Service requirements
for smokejumpers.

Inside, Deanne was ablaze.

She filed a formal complaint
against the Forest Service
based on the Equal Employment
Opportunity Act.
Over the next nine months,
her claim was investigated.

She kept training,
to keep her body strong and ready.
She kept working,
joining a helicopter rappel crew
in Oregon.
She kept listening,
remembering voices of the smokejumpers
who believed in her
as much as she believed in herself.

A response finally came through.
The Forest Service gave her another
chance to become
a smokejumper.
At the age of twenty-eight,
she was allowed
to take all of the tests.

In an Idaho ready room
filled with twelve smokejumpers,
a siren sounded.

Tools were gathered:
McLeods, Pulaskis, shovels, crosscut saws, chain saws.
Personal gear was gathered:
jumpsuits, boots, hard hats, gloves, whistles, fire shelters,
water, and two days of food.

Everything she'd trained with.
Everything needed to slow
the burning of the wildfire
until others could help.

Everything she needed to survive.

Climbing into the plane was easy,
but getting back to the ground . . .

Deanne looked down at the
tall trees far below.

She held tight to the
plane's sturdy door.
Her skin prickled.
Her heart beat as fast as the wind.
She was a little nervous to let go
(but mostly excited).

One, *two*, *three*, she whispered.
And then . . .

she jumped.

AUTHOR'S NOTE

Deanne Shulman made national history by breaking into the ranks of all-male smokejumpers. Because of her efforts, the minimum weight requirement has changed to 120 pounds and the height requirement to five feet. Though Deanne often balks at being labeled a hero, she opened the door of opportunity for all women who work as wildland firefighters.

She jumped a total of seventy-seven times to fight wildland blazes.

In 1994, she applied for a job as a fire-management officer in Los Padres National Forest but lost the role to a less-qualified man. Once again, she filed an EEO complaint against the Forest Service. For three years, she waited for a decision. She eventually won the complaint but chose to work with international forestry programs until her retirement in 2011.

Today she works part-time as a speaker and consultant, using her years of experience to advise emergency-management agencies on systems response to natural disasters and globally recognized best practices and protocols.

On a personal note, Deanne's story is of deep interest to me, and I feel privileged to have interviewed her multiple times in preparation for this book. I've spent a good deal of my life in Colorado, where wildfires are an annual problem, and I learned about wildfires and smokejumpers at a young age. It was part of my daily routine to check the fire danger level on the large sign in my small mountain town.

In my early twenties, I worked with a nonprofit that gave grants to local wildland firefighters. I lived in Colorado during

the Hayman fire in 2002, and my family was very close to being evacuated during the Waldo Canyon fire in 2012. The Black Forest fire that started the following year was devastating to the state as well. I am incredibly grateful to people like Deanne, who fight on the front lines of wildfires to protect our livelihoods.

It must be acknowledged that while wildfire is a natural occurrence, and prescribed, preventative burns are still in use by forest-management agencies, more and more wildfires are ravaging our national forests and those worldwide. Climate change is a factor. Of that, there is no doubt.

GLOSSARY OF TERMS

BRUSH TRUCK: Also known as "wildland engines," these trucks respond to wildfires and have the ability to drive in rough terrain.

CROSSCUT SAW: A saw with a handle at each end, used by two people for cutting across the grain of timber. One-person crosscut saws are also used by the Forest Service.

EQUAL EMPLOYMENT OPPORTUNITY ACT: The Equal Employment Opportunity Act of 1972 is the act that gives the Equal Employment Opportunity Commission (EEOC) authority to sue in federal courts when it finds reasonable cause to believe that there has been employment discrimination based on race, color, religion, sex, national origin, age, disability, or genetic information.

HOTSHOT CREW: In the United States, a hotshot crew, formally known as an interagency hotshot crew, is a hand crew of between twenty and twenty-two wildland firefighters that responds to large high-priority fires across the country and is assigned to work the most challenging parts of the fire. Hotshot crew members are recruited from the strongest wildland firefighters.

McLEOD: A combination of a hoe and rake used especially by the United States Forest Service on the front lines in firefighting.

PULASKI: A chopping and trenching tool widely used in fire-line construction, combining a single-bitted axe blade with a narrow trenching blade fitted to a straight handle.

READY ROOM: The place where smokejumpers take shifts being on call in case they are needed for immediate deployment to a wildfire.

SNOWPACK: Snow that has fallen and does not melt for months due to below-freezing temperatures. During the summer months, a melting snowpack is an important part of both water supply and moisture that can help prevent or lessen the impact of forest fires.

SMOKEJUMPER (alternately, smoke jumper): Smokejumpers are wildland firefighters trained to parachute into fires. They are typically deployed in groups of as few as two and as many as twelve people. The fire crews jump out in pairs, then equipment is sent down after them. The team gathers equipment, works to suppress the fire, then hikes out to an access road where they can be picked up.

WILDLAND CREW: A crew of people sent to deal with the impact of forest fires. Many types of groups fall into this category, including general hand crews, helitack crews (who work with helicopters), hotshot crews, and, of course, smokejumpers.

For Tina —J. L.
For anyone who sets their heart ablaze —S. G.

ADDITIONAL RESOURCE

To learn more about wildfire facts, methods of increasing safety, and decreasing wildfire
risk to homes, visit the National Fire Protection Association website at:
NFPA.org/Public-Education/Fire-Causes-And-Risks/Wildfire/Firewise-USA.

VIKING
An imprint of Penguin Random House LLC
1745 Broadway, New York, New York 10019

First published in the United States of America by Viking, an imprint of Penguin Random House LLC, 2025

Text copyright © 2025 by Jessica Lawson . Illustrations copyright © 2025 by Sarah Gonzales

Visit us online at PenguinRandomHouse.com.

Library of Congress Cataloging-in-Publication Data is available.
ISBN 9780593463659

1 3 5 7 9 10 8 6 4 2

Manufactured in China
TOPL

Edited by Meriam Metoui · Design by Kate Renner and Lily K. Qian · Text set in Circe Slab A

The art for this book was created with watercolor, gouache, colored pencil, and pastel, and was edited digitally.
No AI was used in the creation of this book.